DEDICATION

This book is dedicated to all pastors in the hope that your ministry may be met with great wisdom, insight and readiness to serve God as you love your congregation.

While this book tells the story of a pastor entering into his first church after graduating from seminary, the lessons learned are relevant for any pastor and congregation at any stage of life and ministry.

Therefore this book is also dedicated to every congregation that welcomes their new pastor and every congregation that desires to thrive with their current clergy leader. May you reach out to your pastoral leader with open acceptance, support and a willingness to be led and an eagerness to grow.

Table of Contents

The Effective Servant Leader

Your Role In Nurturing Vital Leadership
In Your Pastor & Congregation

How To Prevent Stress & Anxiety

And Relieve Burnout In Your Church

Reverend Bill McBride

Pastor's Survival Guide

COPYRIGHT

Copyright © Reverend Bill McBride

PUBLISHERS NOTES

Disclaimer

Paperback Edition

ISBN 978-1-944230-02-9 (paperback)

Manufactured in the United States of America

FREE DOWNLOAD

I have a gift set of 4 of my books to give to you today.
Just go to this page & share your email address so I know where to send your 4 book boxed set.

www.ReverendBillMcBride.com/SpiritualityMattersBooks/

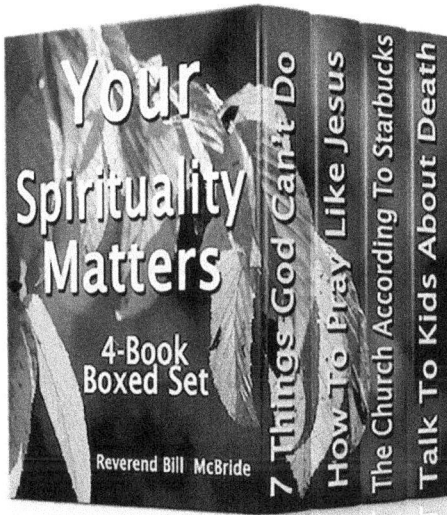

Your spiritual life, faith and growth really matter. Discover deeper insight into your relationship with God and God's love for you as you read this 4-Book Boxed Set.

-"7 Things God Can't Do"
-How To Pray Like Jesus"
-The Church According to Starbucks"
-Talk To Your Kids About Death"

Feel God's presence
Feel inspired to grow in your faith
Get closer to your children
Make a meaningful impact on your church

www.ReverendBillMcBride.com/SpiritualityMattersBooks/

Click this link to get your free books.

FREE DOWNLOAD

5

WELCOME TO
"THE EFFECTIVE SERVANT LEADER"

Author Reverend Bill McBride traces the early ministry of Pastor Wil Bishop to weave a story filled with lessons for life; both for pastors just entering ministry after graduation and for Church members seeking to work well with their current pastor. Using the avenue of religious fiction, Rev. McBride unfolds Pastor Wil Bishop's ministry as he embraces his career, living out his call to preach and teach the Word of God to his people and community.

Through Pastor Wil's trials and temptations, Reverend McBride helps everyday church folks understand and appreciate the local church from the pastor's perspective; a perspective not many people ever see let alone hear about or understand. With humor and heartfelt wisdom, he brings insight and illumination from his many years of parish work throughout Wisconsin. Rev. McBride takes the reader on an eye opening journey of discovery in the local church from the inside out.

While this story is framed in the setting of the United Methodist Church, it speaks to all people involved in the life and ministry of the Church. Rather than a denominational treatise, this book is an exposition of human personality, social and psychological interaction and the expression of one's spiritual motivations and inclinations. Therefore, this book has universal appeal and stands as a helpful tool for pastors and congregations alike.

Reverend William R. McBride is grateful to the members of the congregations he has served and led all across the state of Wisconsin over the past 38 years. Any likeness to real churches and any members of the congregations he has served throughout his ministry is purely coincidental and not intended to judge people or dismiss the important the life lessons he has learned and shares through the main character in The Effective Servant Leader, Pastor Wil Bishop.

CHAPTER 1- FIRST DAY JITTERS

"1 In the beginning God created the heavens and the earth.
2 Now the earth was formless and empty, darkness was over the
surface of the deep, and the Spirit of God was hovering over the
waters."(Genesis 1:1 NIV)

Pastor Wil was on the brink of his new beginning. He opened the door to the incredibly tiny church office in a state of panic. He'd been fearful on many occasions over his past 26 years, but never this scared. Here he was, his first day on the job, in "his" very own church, his books, bibles and supplies still stacked in the moving boxes cluttering his office. Young Pastor Wil had no clue where to begin.

No one told him in theology class what this day would be like. No one ever told him in his psychology of pastoral counseling class what this day would feel like in his gut. Not one of his leaders at the denominational state headquarters, seemingly a million miles south in his hometown of Madison ever warned him what today would feel like deep inside, at the very core of his being. Wil Bishop felt lonely and isolated in his church on this his first day.

Everyone who had taught, supervised and mentored him over the past four years was silent for a good reason. They knew that if they had told him about the numbing panic he would be feeling right now as he stepped from the secure world of seminary into the reality of the church, he'd have bailed out long before he started north on the long trip to his first assignment in this tiny forgotten town of Elk River, population 400.

His heart pounded, his palms sweated and the holy stillness of the tiny empty church building seemed to envelope him and smother him to death. "What in the world am I doing and why in the world am I here?" he kept asking himself. No quick and easy answer came to him today. There was, only the stillness of this holy place interrupted by the beating of his heart deep within his chest.

Wil's office was so small that he could almost reach out with both hands and touch opposite walls. The four walls paneled in cheap fake pine paneling looked stark and ugly. The office desk quietly waiting in the corner for his presence looked metallic, cold and unfriendly; almost appearing like some cast off from a garage sale that no person in the right mind would purchase. Someone must have thought it would serve well in the church, so here it was, "born again" so to speak.

The tiny office window, his only view to the outside world, was dirty and streaked. Apparently no one thought to tidy up the place before he arrived. The shoebox stature of this "Pastor's Office" as the plastic sign tacked above the door outside the office indicated, didn't ease his state of panic at all. All Wil wanted to do at this moment was run as fast as he could from this place and not stop until his was safe again down south at home where he grew up and his parents still lived. Welcome to your own private stained glass jungle Pastor Wil, welcome to church on your first day on the job!

If all this wasn't enough, Wil had moved into this church at mid-week; it was now Wednesday, and he had to be ready for his first Sunday in the pulpit in three days. Three days! "Oh my God," he pleaded under his breath; quickly looking around to make sure no one heard him exclaim. It seemed that Pastor Wil had uttered his first prayer in his first church on his first day and he hardly even noticed he had uttered an honest prayer to His Creator, who at the moment seemed light years away.

Unfortunately, as is the case sometimes when a pastor enters into a new setting, Pastor Wil had no clue where anything was and no one had shown up to give him a personal tour around his church. How easy it would have been for someone, anyone to have met Pastor Wil at church and at least taken five minutes to show him around. He didn't even know where the bathroom was for Pete's sake!

Instead, the president of the Board of Trustees, the group in charge of all church property, had left the church front door key and the office key on his kitchen counter in the church owned house, called the parsonage.

The hand scrawled note taped to the two keys read;

"Welcome to Elk River United Methodist Church. Here are the church keys. If you have any questions give me a call.

Sincerely,

Tom Thompson, Trustee President."

Wil Bishop stood in the middle of his office, took a deep breath and began to wonder about it all. Where are the necessary books, papers, supplies, tools and even where is the stupid bathroom?

Wil had barely three days to get ready for his first public appearance before his congregation. He had learned how to create an order of worship in his worship class in seminary, but no one had taught him the finer details of how to run off the bulletin, how to create and produce announcements and how to select the hymns. His only frame of reference was his home church, Madison United Methodist Church. But Madison Church had 950 members, a full time secretary and the Pastor, Rev. Finch had a staff of 7 to help him with all the details. Here Wil was, in Elk River with 77 members, all alone and he felt completely isolated and lonely.

If all of this wasn't bad enough, another thing that started to eat away at Wil's composure, for which he had no one to blame but himself, was that he could not figure out why he had not written his first sermon before he moved north from his school setting in Kentucky. He had trouble admitting it, but at times like this the truth really hurt more than one cared to admit. "I'll have plenty of time," he remembered telling his mother over the phone as he packed up his last box of stuff from his seminary dorm room, loaded his car to leave town and head back home from school. "Not to worry, mom, I'll get it done."

And now, today in his church office in Elk River he had no clue which box held his favorite Bible study books, his sermon study resources or his collection of prayers. And to make matters even more desperate, Elk River Church had no Internet access, so all his online resources were of no help at all. .

The ingredients for his growing panic rested upon him like a well written recipe Will suddenly realized that he had cooked up a winner of a desert. "Bon appetite, Pastor!"

Young Pastor Wil, barely out of seminary and still soaking wet behind his theological ears, stood paralyzed in his office on this Wednesday morning as his growing anxiety gripped him tightly. All he wanted to do was run and hide. But all that Wil could do in that moment was grit his teeth, close his eyes and take a deep breath. He might have acknowledged if he was in a mood to take a broader theological view of things, that he had just lifted his second desperate prayer to God.

Panic is a strong and potentially dangerous emotion for everyone. One always has two choices in the midst of panic; one to flee and seek escape or two to dig deeper and find an answer and the power to carry on.

Pastor Wil would recall that "first day" on many occasions over his long career. He would come to truly appreciate how much he had learned that first day "on he job" about his humanity, his humility before God and his honest expression of need. He was beginning to learn from the inside out that one cannot undertake any kind of spiritual work without the greater strength and power from a higher place and resource. Pastor Will was already learning some important lessons for his personal and public life. He was gaining that much needed gift of wisdom that would serve him well for years and years to come.

So Pastor Wil opened his eyes that fateful day. He mopped the sweat from his forehead with his shirtsleeve, because no tissue was to be found. He took one more deep breath, walked the two short steps to his far office wall and looked out his tiny office window for the first time. He gazed at the beautiful North Wood's scene of green spring trees, the graceful pines and the newly budding Maples. He marveled at the crystal blue sky enveloping the nature scene. He noticed the early spring Robin's hopping around in search of a worm on the fresh green church lawn.

The words of one of his favorite hymns came back to him and he began to relax and believe. "This is my Father's world, and to my listening ears, all nature rings and loudly signs the music of the spheres."

Wil remembered the real reason he had asked for an assignment way up north when his District Superintendent had queried him as to where in the state he would like to serve if given the chance. He remembered clearly that he'd always wanted to live up in the North Woods among the beauty of God's creation and with a people who were rugged, independent and free of spirit, just like him. And here he finally was, in the place he dreamed, prayed about and sought; now swirling with a heavy dose of down to earth reality.

Wil took one last look out his office window, and then turned to face the boxes of books and papers. He said to himself those words he'd voiced so many times before. They had become his personal mantra and his pledge or token of faith. His words always proved true in his life and he had faith they would prove true again.

   "Not to worry, I'll get it done."

Now, for the first time today, he thought he saw a brief glimmer of light beaming toward him from the sunlit sky outside. The light seemed to penetrate the darkness of his stained glass jungle. He keenly observed this divine light and affirmed his pledge.

   "Not to worry I'll get it done, I'll get it done."

Chapter 1 Words For The Wise

To the Pastor:

- Prepare for your first Sunday in your new church before you get there. (Remember longtime pastor, Sunday is the one day you see most of your congregation. Prepare well in advance.)

- If someone from the church has not set up a tour of the church, initiate that before your first day in the office.

- Put all your needed books and supplies, especially the stuff you will need for your first Sunday in a special box and mark it, so you can get to it as soon as you get to church.

- Assume nothing. The church may not have Internet or other helpful tools you are accustomed to

To the Congregation:

- Have someone meet your pastor at the church on the first day to show him/her around and answer all his/her questions.

- Never assume your pastor knows everything about your congregation policies, procedures and people. Create a resource packet of information you'd like to have if you were the pastor on your first day on the job.

- Personally hand the church keys to your pastor, with a handshake and warm words of welcome. This will go a long way to relieving first day jitters. Say a short prayer with and for your pastor as soon as you arrive at church.

- Put your pastor on your prayer list or prayer chain. Pray for your pastor every day for at least the first year of their ministry among you. (Continue to pray for your current pastor daily.)

- Clean up and spiff up your pastor's office. He/she will spend many hours at church and they deserve a nice place to work.

CHAPTER 2- BAPTISM BY FIRE & WATER

18 Then Jesus came to them and said, "All authority in heaven and on earth has been given to me. 19 Therefore go and make disciples of all nations, baptizing them in the name of the Father and of the Son and of the Holy Spirit, 20 and teaching them to obey everything I have commanded you. And surely I am with you always, to the very end of the age." (Matthew 28:18-20 NIV)

"Hello, is this Pastor Bishop?" queried the polite female voice on the other end of the phone line.

"Yes, Ma'am" responded Wil wanting to sound official but friendly at the same time. "May I help you?"

Wil quickly pulled out a note pad and pen from his desk drawer. He remembered this small piece of advice Rev. Finch had given him just before he left Madison for his drive north. "Whenever the phone rings make sure you have a pen and paper handy. Whoever is calling the church wants something from you and you'd better remember and respond. Remember Wil it is not about you. It is always about them. Trust nothing to memory."

"Pastor, my name is Mary Anderson, you don't know me but I am the mother of your Treasurer Nancy Brown."

Of course Wil didn't know Mary Anderson; he didn't know anyone as of yet for that matter, let alone the mother of one of his members.

"Hello Mary, how can I help you today?"

"Well Pastor," answered Mary, "I know my daughter hasn't had a chance to talk to you yet, but I was wondering if you'd baptize our new granddaughter Eve? Oh, by the way Pastor Bishop, I go to Sacred Heart Church on Elm Street. Have you met our priest Father Hughes? He really is good with the little ones. You'd be impressed with the way he does baptisms at Sacred Heart."

"How nice," scowled Wil. "Now she is setting me up by comparing me to her priest!"

"No Ma'am," answered Wil, as politely as possible, holding back his obvious frustration. "I am sorry, but I have not met Father Hughes, but I will look him up next week".

Fortunately, Wil had unpacked his calendar before he left the parsonage this morning, so he quickly got the conversation back on track by asking Mary, "Do you have any particular questions in mind about the baptism?"

After a brief moment of thought, Mary responded. "We know you are brand new to our little town of Elk River and all and that you just arrived at the church, but I was hoping you could do Eve's baptism this coming Sunday?"

Pastor Will couldn't believe his ears. Is this lady crazy or what? You have got to be kidding me he thought to himself. He took one more deep breath, trying to curb his urge to tell this lady to call him back next month and hang up on her. The nerve of this lady. Doesn't she know I'm new here? Doesn't she care that I hardly know my way around? Does all she care about is her agenda? Then in his most professional pastor voice he said to her, "Mrs. Anderson I have an official policy in the church of setting important dates like baptisms, weddings and other significant family events after I talk directly with the folks most immediately involved, to make sure the date and time are okay first with them. Do you have your daughter's phone number handy so I can call her directly and work out the details with her?"

Wil was drawing upon his wisdom of human behavior. His bachelor's degree in psychology at Madison State University was already coming into play as he suspected it would in his pastoral work. Mary Anderson had tipped her hand by telling him she went to Sacred Heart Church. He knew she probably held her priest in a state of high regard and that she would therefore not press a clergy when they spoke with a tone of official authority.

"Uhh, why yes pastor I do have her phone number," answered Mary rather politely.

"Good, I am ready for the number," said Wil.

After a few more cordial exchanges of words Pastor Wil Bishop told Mary that he would talk with her daughter directly, set an appropriate date for the baptism and get back to her personally as soon as possible. He thanked Mary for calling him with this special family event, congratulated her on the birth of her granddaughter and assured her that he would look forward to meeting her priest very soon.

The second he hung up the phone he reached for his notepad and wrote the following notes:

- Call back to Mary Anderson with details
- Call Nancy Brown, church treasurer about daughter – Eve's baptism
- Mary Anderson – mother Nancy Brown - daughter
- Call Father Hughes – Sacred Heart – next week – Mary Anderson's priest
- Study up on "baptism procedure"!! Important – need help on this one
- Find a baby to practice on
- Find the baptismal font and learn how Elk River UMC does baptisms
- REMEMBER- it's not about you it is always about them

He reviewed his to do list one more time, turned to a fresh sheet of notepad paper, lifted the phone and made his first official pastoral call to the home of his treasurer, Nancy Brown.

Wil's conversation with Nancy Brown was smooth, friendly and informative. He told her that her mother had called about a baptism for Eve. He made a special point to congratulate Nancy on her daughter's birth. He kept especially quiet about his frustrations with Mary and how she had tried to manipulate him by comparing him to Father Hughes.

After a brief chat with Nancy he asked her about a date for Eve's baptism. He made a point to tell Nancy that his policy was always to make plans for a special event with the folks directly involved. He was glad to hear of Mary's desires for the baptism this coming Sunday, but his first priority was to Nancy and her family and he said he'd work hard to make everyone satisfied if possible.

Nancy was quick to apologize for her mother, telling Pastor Wil that Mary had been eager to set up this baptism date as soon as possible because she had waited to get Nancy baptized until Nancy was 10 years old. Mary always felt guilty about waiting so long, especially in the Catholic Church. Nancy told Wil that her mom didn't want her to make the same mistake with her granddaughter.

Nancy thanked Pastor Wil for waiting to set the date until he had talked with her. She reassured Wil that while the family wanted the baptism to take place soon;however, scheduling it for this coming Sunday, Pastor Wil's first Sunday in the pulpit at Elk River Church was not fair to Pastor or the best date for Nancy and her husband and their family.

Wil could not help but realize that the words of the Bible were already coming true in a personal way.

   "Be quick to listen, slow to speak and slow to become angry."

Amen to that he thought to himself.

Nancy said to Wil that she would get back to him next week after she talked with her family, especially her Mom about a good date next month to do the baptism.

 "Sounds good to me," he responded to Nancy as their conversation drew to a close. "I will await your call and seek to keep next month's Sundays open for your family."

"Thanks Pastor Bishop," Nancy said. "I appreciate you calling me so soon after you arrived. I am sorry I didn't call you sooner about Eve's baptism but you now know why my mom was so eager to get it done. Welcome to Elk river and to our church. We are glad you have arrived. We look forward to this Sunday."

It all made sense to Wil as he hung up the phone, closed his note-pad and made a note in the margin of his calendar to "hold the Sundays in June open for the Eve Brown baptism."

"Now" he said to himself, "I guess it's time to find out how to do a baby baptism".

He'd never even held a little baby much less in an official capacity like this. He wished his sister Jennifer, 11 months older and married had decided to have children. It would have been handy to have a niece or nephew to practice on before next month. Maybe he could take out an ad on Craig's List, *"Baby needed to practice on for baptism. Rookie pastor needs your help."* That wouldn't go over well, if his church council found out. Yikes! He'd have to find another way to practice before the big day.

Chapter 2 Words For The Wise

To the Pastor:

- Plan ahead as much as possible. Does the church have official policies for things like baptisms, weddings, funerals etc. (Long time pastor-Keep all important files and documents within easy reach just in case you need them in the future. Never trust such things to your memory.)

- Remember in sales and also in the church-the one who speaks first loses. Always listen a lot and seek to find the reasons why a person is saying and asking to you. (Long Time pastor-Always listen first and speak last.)

- Always have and carry a notebook or pad of paper with you. Be ready to write and take notes whenever someone calls.

- Remember you are a professional, so talk like it and act like it.

To the Congregation:

- Tell your pastor many times in the first month how happy you are that they have come to lead your congregation.

- Let your pastor get settled in for at least two months if possible before you ask for and seek to schedule important family events in the church.

- Seek to be in attendance for your pastor's first three Sundays.

- Let your pastor know in visible ways that you are paying attention to his/her preaching by taking notes and reading along in your Bible.

CHAPTER 3- A BIRD IN THE HAND IS WORTH MORE THAN YOU CAN IMAGINE

5 "On hearing this, they were baptized in the name of the Lord Jesus." (Acts 19:5 New International Version)

On his drive home to the parsonage along the winding county road for a quick lunch and to check on his faithful companion Mittens the cat, Wil kept wondering how he'd handle Eve's baptism. He pulled into the long pine tree-lined driveway, parked his car in front of the garage, got out and started to walk to the back door. He couldn't help but notice the broad expanse of trees lining the property. The church had just recently rented this converted summer cabin on Crystal Lake, so he would have a year round home in Elk River.

Pastor Wil was the first full-time pastor for this congregation. Previously, they had shared a pastor with the United Methodist Church 18 miles south in the town of Minocqua. Wil's residence was nestled up against the Superior National Forest, which suited Wil just fine. Peace and quiet. No neighbors, no highway traffic noise, only the soothing sound of birds, occasional red squirrels and the wind in the pines. He felt lucky to be living up north, even though he was over 300 miles from his hometown and his parents down state.

Just before he climbed the steps to the porch and the entryway he told himself he should find some time every week to get outside and enjoy the beauty of this area. People drove from hundreds of miles around and all the way up from Chicago, just to spend a few days along the trails and fishing in the lakes around Elk River. He'd be real dumb to not get close to this God created beauty himself.

He remembered as a child growing up in Madison, wishing his folks would take a summer vacation up in the north woods. But as far as they ever got was fifty miles north of Madison; and dad thought he was up north! Now he actually lived here. Home sweet home. He was falling in love with Elk River already. A few verses of one of his favorite Psalms came to mind as he stood reverently on his deck in the midst of God's sanctuary and reverently repeated the verses.

1 LORD, our Lord, how majestic is your name in all the earth! You have set your glory in the heavens. 2 Through the praise of children and infants you have established a stronghold against your enemies, to silence the foe and the avenger. 3 When I consider your heavens, the work of your fingers, the moon and the stars, which you have set in place, 4 what is mankind that you are mindful of them, human beings that you care for them?5 You have made them a little lower than the angels and crowned them with glory and honor. 6 You made them rulers over the works of your hands; you put everything under their feet: 7 all flocks and herds, and the animals of the wild, 8 the birds in the sky, and the fish in the sea, all that swim the paths of the seas. 9 LORD, our Lord, how majestic is your name in all the earth! -Psalm 8 (New International Version)

As soon as Wil opened the back door and entered his cabin home he heard the soft meowing of his little cat Mittens. Mittens was his faithful companion ever since he graduated from college and headed to Kentucky for seminary. Mittens already enjoyed her new home up north, eagerly tracking and catching mice for Wil. While Mittens was mostly a house cat, on occasion Wil would let her roam around outside and take in the vast hunting grounds in the woods behind his home.

Mittens was quietly curled up next to the wood stove, absorbing the last bits of heat from the dying embers of this morning's fire.

Part of Wil's desire to live up north was the chance he had to live off the land. He was glad his home had a wood burning stove and a good supply of dry oak and maple stacked neatly along the garage. Even though it was late May and spring was greeting the land, a wood fire was still required in the evening and after rising in the morning just to keep the chill off.

He walked over to Mittens the cat, scratched her behind the ears and carefully picked her up cradling her carefully in his arms. Just a bit over five years of age, Mittens was not a huge cat by any stretch of the word. She weighed in at just over 7 pounds, the size of a newborn baby. Then with a startled impulse of inspiration Wil thought of little Eve Brown, probably not weighing much more than Mittens. Mittens the cat, like a little baby in his arms; Eve Brown a real life newborn baby soon to be in his arms. What if I practice on Mittens?

Wil gently laid Mittens back on the rug by the wood stove. Mittens gave out a soft purr of approval. "Mittens my friend, I think I've found someone to help me get ready for the baptism." Mittens the cat would do nicely to help Pastor Wil practice his baptism skills as he anticipated holding little Eve in his arms for the very first time.

"Mittens you are in for some fun; but I promise I won't use real water on your little head. Extra treats for you tonight Mittens if you help me out. But you have to promise never to tell anyone I practiced on you before my first baptism at Elk River United Methodist Church."

As Wil walked over to the refrigerator to get out the ingredients for his usual peanut butter and jelly sandwich, he felt a sense of relief in knowing he'd not have to do his first baptism without a way to practice first. Wil felt a smooth sense of smug satisfaction and confidence at having initially solved his baptism dilemma.

Almost without hesitation, the shocking reality hit him again, here it was Wednesday noon and he had to write a sermon, prepare the Sunday worship bulletin, pick the hymns, talk to the organist and find a way to get everything ready; all of this in three days.

Wow! Time to get back to work.

Chapter 3 Words For The Wise

To the Pastor:

- Time off to rest and renew are essential to your strength and leadership. You need at least one or two days off a week. Schedule them and take them religiously.

- Find creative ways to "practice before you preach." When it comes to doing things in public, you want to look as competent and professional as you can.

- Never let on or say "I am real new and not sure of myself here,"or "I've never done this before." Your congregation wants to believe they are making a good investment in your leadership. Your confidence will go a long way to building trust and helping them to relax with you.

To the Congregation:

- Respect your pastor's need for space and privacy. He/she understands that they are on duty 24/7 especially in times of your need. Just like you, your pastor needs time away from work to rest, relax and renew.

- Try not to assume that Sunday is a time of worship for your pastor just as it is for you. Sunday is your pastor's most visible time with the congregation. They are helping you worship most of all. Sunday is always a work day for your pastor.

- Encourage your pastor to take at least 2 days off per week. Most folks in the congregation have Saturday and Sunday off, so why not the pastor have two days too?

CHAPTER 4- A PULPIT IS MUCH MORE THAN A 'SERMON HOLDER'

"Preach the word; be prepared in season and out of season; correct, rebuke and encourage—with great patience and careful instruction." (2 Timothy 4:2)

All through seminary Wil Bishop heard about the wonderful and talented preaching professor by the name of Dr. Ron Joy. Dr. Joy was also the chair of the seminary drama department, so it stood to reason that he'd know something about preaching. And know something he certainly did.

Of all his coursework Wil really enjoyed his preaching classes. He rather liked being up on stage, having sung in the high school glee club and played in the concert band. But now he had the fine opportunity to learn the skills of preaching, of taking a Bible text or story and opening it up before his congregation. Now this week, he was honestly looking forward to his first Sunday in the pulpit. The only thing that stood in his way was coming up with something worthwhile and important to say.

As soon as he arrived back at church from his lunch break, he unlocked his office put down his Bible on the desk and made his way into the worship area and walked up the three steps to the platform and stood behind the pulpit. Here he was for the first time, standing in his sanctuary, in his pulpit looking out toward the pews where his congregation would gather on Sunday morning at 9:00am.

Then, something odd started to happen. Wil Bishop's, legs began to quiver and his knees started to knock. He felt weak and wobbly like a groom about to say his vows. The longer Wil stood there, gazing out into the sanctuary the more nervous he became. While he had done quite well in preaching class at school, being graded in the top five of his class; that being a good mark considering his grade came from the head of the drama department and also the classmates grading each other. Right now, on this day, Wednesday afternoon, standing in the pulpit of Elk River United Methodist

Church, he seriously thought he might faint and fall over. And so he did what any sane person would do, he grabbed the sides of the sturdy wood pulpit and he hung on for all he was worth. A pulpit is more than a sermon holder; today it was a pastor holder too. Pastor Wil Bishop with all his training, and study and even a sermon or two preached at school was very much afraid. Another dose of humility took him by the nape of his neck and he consciously said a desperate prayer.

"God, I really need your help this Sunday, if I am going to get through my first service."

He remembered his pastor back home telling him one afternoon that the people of the church want and expect their pastor to walk, talk, act and preach like he or she has it all together and knows exactly what needs to be done.

"So Wil," his pastor and mentor said, "My advice to you when you get started up at Elk River is to never let them see you sweat. Fake it if you have to, until you make it and figure it out."

Wil remembered the well-turned phrase of the founder of his denomination, John Wesley who once said, "Preach faith until you have it."

Well, thought Wil, preach until you figure it out and hang on tight to the pulpit, lest you fall over and embarrass yourself. Wil took a deep breath, seems like there was a lot of deep breathing going on this first day, and he quietly walked out of the sanctuary and headed down the short hall to his tiny office. He settled in behind his desk in the creaky wood chair, obviously another garage sale reject. He began to look for his study books and his sermon preparation tools. It's time to prepare my message. I haven't a moment to lose.

Chapter 4 Words To The Wise

To the Pastor:

- Get to know your pulpit well ahead of your first Sunday. You will be spending a lot of time there, so get comfortable.

- Give yourself plenty of time to practice before Sunday. Be in control of as many variables as possible.

- If the furniture in the office does not suit you or meet your needs, talk to the Trustees, the building care group about something else. Be prepared to purchase your own desk and chair with your own money. That way you can get what you really want. Find out how the current equipment got to the office and if any one has any reason why it cannot be replaced.

To the Congregation:

- Take care of the pastor's office and administrative needs as best as you can.

- Churches sometimes end up being great places for cast off furniture and equipment. If you would not want or use a certain item in your own home, then probably it would not be a good idea to give it to the church.

- If your church does not have secretary on staff, try to find competent volunteers to assist your pastor right from the start.

- Remember your pastor on special occasions, birthday, anniversary of their coming to your church and at Christmas time.

CHAPTER 5- THE DAY BEFORE
THE BIG DAY

" 22-25So let's do it—full of belief, confident that we're presentable inside and out. Let's keep a firm grip on the promises that keep us going. He always keeps his word. Let's see how inventive we can be in encouraging love and helping out, not avoiding worshiping together as some do but spurring each other on, especially as we see the big Day approaching." (Hebrews 10:25 The Message)

On Saturday morning Pastor Wil got up early. He wanted to practice his sermon for his first Sunday in church. He really didn't know if any members would be around church on Saturday, so he hoped to get there early enough and have some practice time alone.

When Wil got up, Mittens was already roaming around the kitchen looking for her morning bowl of cat food. Wil had a daily ritual that always involved taking care of Mittens, a fresh cup of coffee and devotions with the Upper Room electronic edition on his iPhone.

He appreciated his hometown friend Mark Hoggarty for recommending this email version of the Upper Room. It was waiting in his email inbox everyday and was the first thing he did after getting up and settling into his favorite chair with his first cup of coffee.

He was glad that his home had Internet access because his life line to family and friends and his ready access to online preaching and study resources depended on his ability to get to the Internet. He hoped that one day soon his church would get into the 21st century and provide Internet too. He would have to learn that old adage "If you want something to take a long time to happen, give it to a church committee to figure out." He wanted to ask them right away to provide it, but he hadn't figured out quite yet how to ask and whether it is best to wait for a time later on. He didn't realize it now, but later on, after many years in the ministry he would know how to skillfully balance urgency and timing in the life and leadership of the church. For now, he'd have to do his online research from the comfort of his parsonage home.

After feeding Mittens, putting a few more logs in the wood burning stove and gathering all his books, calendar, study Bible and papers he set off to church. Time to practice and get ready for the big day tomorrow.

When Wil arrived at church, the small parking lot on the west side of the building was empty. He breathed a sigh of relief. He stood a good chance of not being interrupted as he practiced his sermon. He unlocked the door and made his way in the dim light of day-break up the four steps to his office. Unlocking the door, he again said out loud, "starting next week, first thing, I have to get my books and stuff organized. But now it's time to practice."

Wil opened the door and walked into his sanctuary area. He only turned on the lights that illuminated the altar and pulpit area. He didn't want to alert anyone who might be driving by to stop and investigate why all the church lights were on at this early time of the morning. He opened his folder and practiced until he almost knew his sermon by heart.

He left the sanctuary headed for his office and started to create the bulletin, the order of worship. He had some experience with doing this, for in his worship class at seminary each student had to create and share a liturgy with the class. He powered up his computer, found the liturgy he had created in school, made a few changes and went to print for tomorrow's worship time.

Fortunately in his wandering around the church he found a copy machine down in the basement in a little room next to the church kitchen. There was a stake of white paper next to the machine with a note on top of the paper. It said, "Run off 65 copies each Sunday for worship." How about that one, thought Wil, finally some helpful advice from someone.

He ran off 75 copies, anticipating a few extra curious members would show up to check out the new pastor. He folded the bulletins headed back upstairs and packed up his books and computer. It was just about 7:00am and he was done for the day.

He decided to head downtown, just three blocks from church and grab a coffee at the local restaurant. Time to say hello to a few towns' folks. The restaurant on the main street had a curious name. "The Duck Shack." The parking lot was almost full with just one spot left. He parked his car and headed inside. "We'll see if any one notices the new guy in town." He felt good to be here and to have himself almost all ready for tomorrow's service.

No sooner did he settle into the corner booth then a man came up to him from behind the counter. He stopped right in front of Wil, gave him a long look, gave out a smile and said, "Well hello, you look new in town, can I get you a cup of coffee?"

"Yes please", said Wil."

"What brings you to Elk River young man?", asked the waiter as he turned to get him his coffee?

"I'm the new pastor, Wil Bishop at the Methodist Church up the block," answered Wil.

The man took a longer look at Wil, gave out a bigger smile, reached out his hand and said, "Well, I'll be damned. Our new pastor has finally made it to the Duck Shack. Hey everybody, meet Wil Bishop my new pastor."

Wil was just a bit taken back by such a cheerful welcome and meeting one of his church members too.

"Pastor Wil, I'm John Wilpont. I run this here Duck Shack and I am really pleased to meet you this nice spring day. Hang on, I'll be right back with your coffee."

Wil sat back in his seat, trying not to feel so conspicuous; but he couldn't help notice that most all the folks at the Duck Shack this morning were checking him out and chatting back and forth with each other. He wondered if any other of the people there were his members as well.

Wil would soon learn that being a pastor in a small town the likes of Elk River was almost like being a fish in a fishbowl. It wasn't long before John came back with his cup of steaming coffee and a plate with a fresh cinnamon roll.

 "Here at the Duck Shack Saturdays are famous for my homemade cinnamon rolls. I thought you might like one today, this one's on me. Enjoy," said John.

Wil sat back and thought to himself as he gazed at the enormous cinnamon roll gracing the plate. The warm aroma of the roll and the sight of a pad of melting butter atop the roll made him feel glad. "I guess there are some benefits to being a pastor in Elk River after all," thought Wil.

The rest of Wil's day was uneventful and quiet. He spent some time organizing his study and bookshelf at the parsonage and later in the afternoon took Mittens outside for a time of hunting and relaxing. Wil knew he'd better get to bed early tonight, for tomorrow would be a big day.

CHAPTER 6- FIRST SERMON AT ELK RIVER UNITED METHODIST CHURCH

Genesis 17:1-8, 15-16; 18:1-5

1-2 When Abram was ninety-nine years old, GOD showed up and said to him, "I am The Strong God, live entirely before me, live to the hilt! I'll make a covenant between us and I'll give you a huge family."

3-8 Overwhelmed, Abram fell flat on his face. Then God said to him, "This is my covenant with you: You'll be the father of many nations. Your name will no longer be Abram, but Abraham, meaning that 'I'm making you the father of many nations.' I'll make you a father of fathers—I'll make nations from you, kings will issue from you. I'm establishing my covenant between me and you, a covenant that includes your descendants, a covenant that goes on and on and on, a covenant that commits me to be your God and the God of your descendants. And I'm giving you and your descendants this land where you're now just camping, this whole country of Canaan, to own forever. And I'll be their God."

15-16 God continued speaking to Abraham, "And Sarai your wife: Don't call her Sarai any longer; call her Sarah. I'll bless her—yes! I'll give you a son by her! Oh, how I'll bless her! Nations will come from her; kings of nations will come from her."

1-2 GOD appeared to Abraham at the Oaks of Mamre while he was sitting at the entrance of his tent. It was the hottest part of the day. He looked up and saw three men standing. He ran from his tent to greet them and bowed before them.

3-5 He said, "Master, if it please you, stop for a while with your servant. I'll get some water so you can wash your feet. Rest under this tree. I'll get some food to refresh you on your way, since your travels have brought you across my path." They said, "Certainly. Go ahead."

Sermon Title: **"How To Have a New Beginning"**

Theme: *"God is always the God of new beginnings. How we experience our new beginnings gives a witness to our faith and trust in God and sets the stage for our journey along the way."*

Once upon a time there was a couple that was about to have a new beginning. As they considered this new beginning, they did what many folks do when faced with the prospect of such an experience, They:

- wondered,
- asked questions,
- felt a few doubts framed by their dreams and a promise.

Being people of faith, their planning and preparing also included discovering God's will for their lives. And so they were ready and they moved ahead into their new beginning.

How do You Have a New Beginning?

The Bible starts with beginnings and new beginnings. The Book of Genesis means "Beginnings" Genesis 17& 18 – is the story about Abraham and Sarah in their new beginning.

Here we are today at church with this new beginning. This is your first Sunday on your own with a full time pastor. You are no longer linked with another church in another town. You asked for a full time pastor for your very own because you had faith and belief that this was a good idea, a dream given by your Creator and here we are together in this new beginning.

Today is a new beginning for me as your pastor. The classes, the tests, the papers and the life in seminary far away in Kentucky are now memories. I asked for a church in the north woods and I am here by appointment of our bishop and by the choosing of God. In your personal lives this week maybe you are in the midst of a new beginning or two. May we seek to view our lives in terms of a new beginning for the scriptures are instructive in this regard?

Your New Beginning is a fresh start, something you are a part of;

your relationships, your family, your work, your health and your church can all be understood in this way.

New beginnings have a way of finding us and challenging us don't they? A New Beginning found, challenged and tested Abram and Sarai one day.

When we face a new beginning it changes us. For the better? For the wiser? For the Worse? The choice is ours in terms of what we do and how we move into and with our new beginning. Are we becoming better people because of our new beginnings? Time will tell for sure.

Think about Abraham and Sarah. Do you ever wonder why God changed their names? The way it appears in the Bible was not a typo. I suspect it was to inform them and the reader that when you have a new beginning you change and you are different than before. AND YOUR NEW BEGINNING does not have to be threatening or bad or destructive.

Abraham and Sarah teach us two things. We learn how we can grow as we begin in this church with our new pastor and as we seek to make the most out of our lives.

IN YOUR NEW BEGINNINGS SEEK ALWAYS TO:
1-Honor God and
2-Have a Plan.

This is How to have a New Beginning.

Our time this morning does not permit me to go into very much detail on our plan for the days, months and years ahead. In one way this is good because this beginning is OUR new beginning and we each have a stake in how it is developed and how it comes to pass. I encourage you to reread and think about Abraham and Sarah tonight.

HOW TO HAVE A NEW BEGINNING?

FIRST- HONOR GOD

- Walk blameless with God
- See yourself as a servant
- Be eager to meet God everyday
- Act humbly before God
- Give hospitality to other people around you, they might just be angels in your midst AND
- Be ready for God's unfolding plan in and for your life.

SECOND- HAVE A PLAN (God's plan)

- God confirms his promises (covenant)
- God changes us for the better so to serve him and each other
- God makes us fruitful inside and outside the church
- God blesses us in unimaginable ways
- Abraham and Sarah obeyed the plan.

This is how we have a new beginning as God's wonderful people in our everyday lives and relationships.

How will you grow in your life this week in light of God's call to honor the Creator and follow God's plan? (CHALLENGE FOR YOU)

Allow me to share a brief summary of our theme this week with my take on our New Beginning.

1. God has a great plan for our life together in this church (always has and always will). We just have to walk willingly and eagerly with God and help God's plan unfold.
2. God has been by your sides all along and has never and will never leave you alone or lonely. (God is right here, right now and it is my calling as your pastor to never let you forget that Good News)
3. God calls us as a body of faith, the church family, to look for God's presence in our midst and in each other. (IT IS PART OF MY PLAN AS YOUR PASTOR TO CATCH YOU DOING THINGS RIGHT)

4. God will always honor us and bless us when we organize well, plan carefully and communicate clearly with each other.

This is how to have a new beginning.

How will your NEW BEGINNING go this week?

Amen

Author's Note:
We leave pastor Wil as he finishes his first service of worship at his first church on his first Sunday of the first week in his pastoral career.

I hope this story has helped you whether you are a new pastor, a clergy person involved in your calling of many years or a church member who is engaged in the life and ministry of your church.

Please show your faithful support for your pastor. They work hard and go without many of life's comforts as they seek to care for you and help your church thrive.

Sometimes, the best things are the small heartfelt things given to your pastor to show your appreciation: a thank you card with a personal note of appreciation, a holiday gift and a special something for "Pastor Appreciation Month."

May God guide you in your ministry in your church.

Blessings,

Reverend Bill McBride

ABOUT THE AUTHOR

Reverend William Robert (Bill) McBride graduated from the University of Wisconsin, Madison campus with a Bachelor's Degree in Psychology, followed by a Master's Degree in Theology from the Asbury Theological Seminary in Kentucky.

His is currently pursuing a PhD in Metaphysics through the American Institute of Holistic Theology and enjoys writing spiritual books that endeavor to help people grow in their faith and spiritual living.

Reverend McBride has served as a church pastor for over 38 years. He entered ministry in the late 1970's in Northern Wisconsin, after his three year training in a Christian seminary in Kentucky, USA.

FREE DOWNLOAD

I have a gift set of 4 of my books to give to you today.
Just go to this page & share your email address so I know where to
send your 4 book boxed set.

www.ReverendBillMcBride.com/SpiritualityMattersBooks/

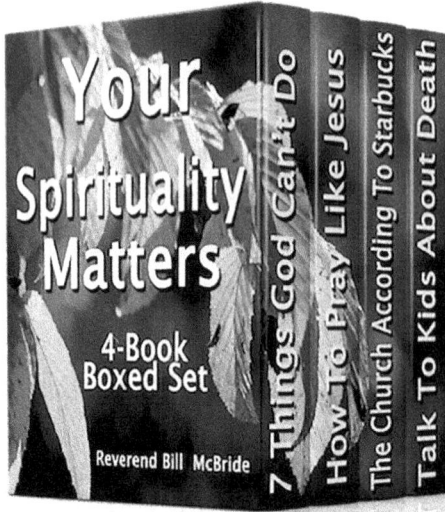

Your spiritual life, faith and growth really matter. Discover deeper
insight into your relationship with God and God's love for you as you
read this 4-Book Boxed Set.

-"7 Things God Can't Do"
-How To Pray Like Jesus"
-The Church According to Starbucks"
-Talk To Your Kids About Death"

Feel God's presence
Feel inspired to grow in your faith
Get closer to your children
Make a meaningful impact on your church

www.ReverendBillMcBride.com/SpiritualityMattersBooks/

Click this link to get your free books.

FREE DOWNLOAD

Energizing Church Leadership And Administration

Learn how to help your church reach new levels of growth and vitality. Effective tools to assess & implement change.

★ ★ ★ ★ ★ 1 ratings, 33 students enrolled

Instructed by Reverend Bill McBride   Business / Management

$SPECIAL DISCOUNT

Take This Course

Redeem a Coupon
Start free preview
More options ▾

Lectures	58
Video	4 Hours
Skill level	All level
Languages	English
Includes	Lifetime access
	30 day money back guarantee!
	Available on iOS and Android
	Certificate of Completion

♡ Wishlist

Course Description

If you pray for and desire a vibrant church, If you want to turn around your decline, if you want innovative and easy to follow methods to reach out to new people, this course is for you.

The course offers short videos, downloadable mp3 audios for listening when away from your computer, PDF document files and a comprehensive assessment tool for use in every local church setting.

Also included is a detailed mind-map of the entire lecture themes contained in the course.

This course is a detailed "How To Manual" that follows the teachings of the instructor's Kindle book, "The Church According To Starbucks: Radical Hospitality For Growing a Healthy Church."

I have a special 25% discount for you as a thank you for purchasing this book. Use the link below and click the "Redeem Coupon" button and enter the code - "**Pastor**."

http://bit.ly/1S7k9gC **Use this link for your discount**

www.ingramcontent.com/pod-product-compliance
Lightning Source LLC
Chambersburg PA
CBHW071800020426
42331CB00008B/2338